John Wright is an award-winning international teacher and theatre-maker. He is a former student of Jacques Lecoq, Monika Pagneux and Philippe Gaulier and a former teacher at Gaulier's school in London.

He co-founded Trestle Theatre Company in 1980 and Told by an Idiot in 1990. He has a string of productions and projects extending over three decades in Europe, Scandinavia, Asia and the UK. John's work has made innumerable contributions to the Edinburgh Festival Fringe. He won a Fringe First for *Aesop* (National Youth Music Theatre), the Peter Brook Award for *Dr Faustus* (Third Party Productions), the Spirit of the Fringe Award for *The Fragility of X* (Coal Theatre) and the Summerhall Award for *Lost in Blue* (Debs Newbold). In addition, he's made a specialist contribution to productions at the National Theatre, the RSC, the Royal Court, the Almeida and the Royal Opera House.

John was granted a Greater London Arts Award for his contribution to professional training; and his belief that teaching is the greatest source of learning has enabled his ideas to be shaped and moulded by generations of students with an open mind and an insatiable curiosity. He pioneered the teaching of Clown at university level and was one of the first people in the country to offer courses in devising.

His work with masks and physical comedy has contributed to the making of *Rain Dance* (Chicago Rep), *Rhinoceros* (Royal Court), *Macbeth* (Chichester Festival Theatre), *Laurel and Hardy* and *Arabian Nights* (Victoria Theatre, Stoke-on-Trent), *Endgame* (Liverpool Playhouse), *The Last Days of Judas Iscariot, American Psycho* and *Medea* (Almeida).

His book *Why Is That So Funny?* (Nick Hern Books) is immensely popular, and is also published in Romania and the USA. His TEDx Talk *Discovering Playfulness in Acting* can be viewed at youtu.be/KjulpNLzYNc.

At the time of writing John is working on a clown show with Frank Wurzinger about narcissism called *Me Me Me*, and a project on *Hamlet* with Debs Newbold, that will look at Hamlet through the eyes of Gertrude.

Also by John Wright

WHY IS THAT SO FUNNY?
A Practical Exploration of Physical Comedy

JOHN WRIGHT

PLAYING THE MASK

Acting Without Bullshit

Foreword by Paul Hunter

NICK HERN BOOKS

London

www.nickhernbooks.co.uk

A Nick Hern Book

Playing the Mask: Acting Without Bullshit
first published in Great Britain in 2017
by Nick Hern Books Limited
The Glasshouse, 49a Goldhawk Road, London W12 8QP

Cover: Naomi Ackie as Arlecchino, photo by Toby Wright
Author photo: Robert Golden
All mask photos: Toby Wright

Designed and typeset by Nick Hern Books
Printed and bound in Great Britain
by Ashford Colour Press, Gosport, Hampshire

A CIP catalogue record for this book
is available from the British Library

ISBN   978 1 85459 580 5

*This book is dedicated to the mask-maker
Ninian Kinnier-Wilson, who died in 2013.*

*Without his perception and skill as a mask-maker
this work would have been impossible.*

Contents

Foreword by Paul Hunter — xiii

Preface — xv

Acknowledgements — xviii

1. Raking Over a Few Gurus — 1

Rules — 6

The Way We Learn — 7

The Dreyfus Brothers — 8

Big-Boy Stan — 11

Copeau and the Mask — 12

The 'Ten Commandments' — 13

Moshe Feldenkrais — 16

In the Beginning was the Mask… — 18

   The Handkerchief Game — 19

   The Spectacles Game — 21

The Tomato-Sandwich Incident — 27

'The Holy Trinity' — 32

   'Have nothing to remember' — 33

   'Finding the game' — 38

   'Suck it and see' — 43

The Only Rule of Theatre — 45

2. When the Whole Face is Covered: Playing Full-Mask — 47

Ko–omote — 49

How Masks Work — 51

   The Face-Match Game — 55

The Eyes or Mouth Debate — 56

   The Smile Game — 58

Trigger-Lines   59
Project Bali   60
Woman About To Do Something   64
The Politics of Beauty   67
The Quest for Symmetry   69
Playing Neutral   70
   Playing Tag   70
   The Heavy-Arms Game   73
Where Sculpture and Acting Meet   74
   The Pygmalion myth   76
The Innocent   78
The Archetype of Play   80
Playing an Impulse   81
   The Shoe Game   81
Playfulness   84
My Great Gaffe   85
The Mechanics of Play   86
   The Innocent's Game   86
Nice-but-Dim   90
   The Play Game   91
The Determined Heron   93
   The Paper-Bag Game   94
   The Flirting Game   95
   The Presents Game   97
Counter-Mask (1)   100
A Difficult Commission   102
Woman About To Be Hero   103
Composite Types   104
   The Physiognomy Game   104
The Hero   108
Pure Types and Composite Types   110
A Break with Tradition   113
   The Back-to-Back Game   114
   Playing Blind   114
   The Morning-After-the-Night-Before Game   119

3. When Part of the Face is Covered: 121
   Playing Half-Mask

Arlecchino   123
The Arlecchino Mask   125
The Powerhouse of the Mask   126
    The Half-Mask Face-Match Game   129
    The Prompting Game   130
    The Rhythm Game   133
Animal Motifs   134
Playing the Provocateur   136
    The Slapstick Game   136
    The Dog-Training Game   138
Direct Provocation   140
    The Blocking Game   141
    The Dog-Handler Game   142
Mr Magoo (The Modern Half-Mask)   145
Modern Half-Masks and Connected Speech   149
    The Speech-Impediment Game   152
    The Expert Game   153
Mutual Provocation   154
Man Trying To Be Nice (Balinese Bondres)   157
Counter-Mask (2)   159
    The Lying Game   162
Between the Shape and the Person   163
The Red Nose (The Smallest Mask in the World)   166
The Blood Orange Story   167
The Nose Incident   168
The Big Lesson   170
A Little Neutral Mask for the Clown   175
    The Stopping-and-Starting Game   175
    The Horizon Game   177
    The Inappropriate-Text Game   179

4. When the Mask Becomes a Thought: 181
   Archetypal Masks

The Trickster   185
    The Archetype Game   186
Mirror Neurons   188

The Trickster's Game   191
A List of Masks and Their Trigger-Lines   192
The Trigger-Line Game   193
'Persona' and 'Character'   194
Man About To Be Hero   197
The Hero   199
The Persona Game   201
Ninian's Archetypal Masks   202
The Fool   206
The Fool's Game   207
The Victim   209
The Victim's Game   210
The Game of Chase   211
The Topping-It Game   211
The Child   213
The Child's Game   214
The Virgin   216
The Virgin's Game   218
The Mother   219
The Mother's Game   221
The Huntress   223
The Huntress's Game   225
The Ogre   226
The Ogre's Game   227
The Crone   228
The Crone's Game   230
The Hermit   231
The Hermit's Game   233
The Devil   236
The Devil's Game   237
The Size Game   239

5.   When the Text Becomes a Mask   241
Lady Macbeth in Feathers   243
The Tape Game   246
The Interloper   247
The first version   248
The Positive-Feedback Game   249

The second version 250
Coping with the Gap 251
The third version 252
The fourth version 254
The Choice of Text 256
Listening 257
The Listening Game 258
The Scarf Game 259
The Liking-and-Loathing Game 261
The Opposites Game 262
Using Archetypes 264
An Afternoon with the Macbeths 264
Playing Blind and the Tape Game 266
Romeo as The Devil 268
Simple Provocations 269
Using Half-Masks 271
The Grunting-and-Heavy-Breathing Game 272
Using Neutral Mask 275
The Times-Table Game 276
Angles of Expression 279
Using Clown 281
Finding the Game 282
The Pause Game 284

In Conclusion: Something for Tomorrow 289

Foreword
Paul Hunter

I first encountered John Wright and his teaching when I arrived as a naive would-be actor at Middlesex Polytechnic in 1986. I embarked on my Diploma in Dramatic Art with very little notion of what acting actually was. Save for a few visits as a teenager to Stratford-upon-Avon and watching Danny La Rue in *Mother Goose*, my experience of observing live performance was fairly limited.

I could only have been at college a matter of weeks when I found myself in front of my peers, being questioned by John in an improvisation class.

'What are you doing?' John enquired in a rather provocative manner.

'Er, what you asked me to do,' I replied, losing my confidence by the second.

'No, I mean: what are you doing?' John insisted. By now I was confused.

'Er… I… was… doing what you asked me to do.'

This faltering exchange, it seemed to me, went on for some time, although it couldn't have been that long before John finally said, to the sound of titters from my fellow students, 'You're standing there like some idea of a classical actor, but you're a short bloke from Birmingham. You should concentrate on being *that*.'

Mortified as I was at the time, and unable to articulate exactly why, I began to find John and his teaching fascinating. A small group of us walked up North End Road week after week to a movement, mask or improvisation class, feeling the perfect mix of fear and excitement.

John's honesty and playfully mischievous approach remain intact thirty years later, and his insight into not just masks but theatre in general shines through in this extraordinary book. An ongoing curiosity and fascination with spontaneity has made John a unique presence in British theatre.

I have lost count of the number of occasions I have been in a workshop or rehearsal room and witnessed performers in a mask being provoked by John. Time and again they play and invent in a way that has taken themselves and the audience completely by surprise. This is not to be underestimated. John's ability to help actors be present – utterly in the moment – is a rare quality in a teacher or director. As this book illustrates, this is all done with a rigour, a lightness of touch, and the perfect balance of taking the work seriously – but never himself.

John continues to explore masks to develop ideas and ask questions, never to find answers or solve problems. There is no mystique for him, and in reading this book I am reminded of those early days, wearing a half-mask and being provoked by John.

The utter liberation I felt in being 'put in the shit' by a safe pair of hands, and realising I could simply make it up, was like someone opening a door for me.

I know John has opened doors for many actors, writers and directors over the years, and this brilliant, entertaining and accessible new book will no doubt find him new followers.

Playing the Mask is that rare achievement: a theatre book that transcends its topic and is written exactly how its author speaks. As a teacher and director, John has always been unorthodox, unconventional and non-conformist. He is a true maverick, who never stands still, remains as passionate as ever, and continues to find laughter in the unlikeliest of places.

Paul Hunter is co-founder (with Hayley Carmichael and John Wright) and Artistic Director of Told by an Idiot. He made his stage debut in a talent competition at The Cliff Caff Club in Margate in 1973 singing Slade's 'Cum On Feel the Noize'.

Preface

We tend to see the word 'bullshit' as an expletive, at best a vulgar Americanism, but it's a word that's passed into the English vernacular. 'Bullshit' is a recognised word. *The Concise Oxford English Dictionary* tells us that the word 'bullshit' means 'to talk nonsense in order to deceive'. But in acting, the biggest lie becomes the greatest truth, and deception is endemic. The ever-popular notion that you must know exactly what you're going to do before you do it is bullshit. Similarly, the assertion that the more lifelike you are, the more credible you're going to be, is also bullshit. Mask-work flies directly in the face of both these ideas, but mask-work also comes with even more bullshit of its own. Arcane beliefs that masks induce trance and possession are prime bullshit and they do nothing to inspire us to use masks in the first place.

Playing the Mask: Acting Without Bullshit is about masks: what they do, how they do it, and above all what they teach us about acting. It's an attempt to demystify what happens when you play a mask, and to offer a more realistic approach to acting and textual interpretation.

The ideas and processes described here aren't necessarily easier or more effective than the more traditional acting techniques that the vast majority of us have been brought up on. Traditional training is concerned with responsible and accurate interpretation, rather than playfulness. But playfulness generates ideas, finds meaning and is infinitely more fun to do. The ideas in this book aren't 'new', or 'better' than any other ideas about acting. There is no 'right' or 'wrong' in art. I'm simply offering something else: something different, something to fire your imagination in a different way, or in a way that you might have tried before but subsequently dropped, for reasons best known to yourself. Mask-work doesn't require you to reject everything that's gone before. After all, once psychology's out of the box, you'll never get it back in again. But research in psychology and developments in neuroscience have completely changed the landscape, and change the way we look at acting since Stanislavsky's day.

Enquiry is more acceptable in actor training today than it was even a decade ago. I meet more and more practitioners who are interested in posing questions rather than making categorical statements about the work they do. *Playing the Mask: Acting Without Bullshit* is an attempt to feed your curiosity and nudge you into trying things out for yourself.

I'm not proselytising here. Playing a mask won't change your life or get you into Heaven, but it might open a door into a fascinating place entirely of your own creation. Good experiences encourage us to return to things that have worked in the past. But if you do that all the time as a performer, we the audience will all die of boredom. I haven't met any skilled and experienced actors who work the way they were trained to work in drama school. We all have to find our own way in the end, and we do this more by trial and error than by following a particular creed.

The trouble is that theatre, like any other industry, is deeply conservative in its understanding of process. Practitioners refute any implication that they're remotely conservative, of course. After all, they're artists, and no artist wants to be branded as 'conservative'. But industry is shaped by money, and the desire to make money promotes processes that best fit the industry, and this in turn cultivates a taste for actor training that feeds the demands of industry, as opposed to art.

Ultimately, *Playing the Mask: Acting Without Bullshit* is a book about process in training and theatre-making. It isn't a book about making masked theatre, or traditional masked-theatre forms and their various historical manifestations. You'll find an eclectic and pragmatic approach to mask-work here. I don't care where a mask comes from or what it was originally intended to do. For me, masks are devices that inspire specific qualities of play. The leading question is: What will that mask inspire you to do?

In this world you might find Lady Macbeth being played in the **Red Nose** of the Clown, or Hamlet in the mask of **The Victim**, **The Ogre** or **The Fool**. You might even find Romeo and Juliet playing in grotesque half-masks. You won't see any of this in the final production, but, in rehearsal, work like this informs what you might do in the end, whether you're working with the linguistic complexity of a Shakespeare play or the inanity of a commercial voice-over. Whatever the material you're working with, masks are empowering: they encourage you to delegate responsibility. They enable you to take risks. They provoke you into working with the reckless logic of a six-year-old or the enigmatic stillness of someone wiser than you'll ever be. But above all, masks let you be *you* without your habitual limitations.

John Wright

Acknowledgements

My initial thanks are to my wife, Mary, without whose continuing support this project would have been impossible, and also to my son Toby and daughter-in-law Pippa. I am indebted to them all for their help and their patience. I would also like to thank Victoria Worsley, Debs Newbold and Joey Robinson-Holden, who read parts of the text in its early stages.

But this book would simply not have happened were it not for the playfulness and curiosity of generations of actors and acting students who have provoked and fed my imagination over the years, and whose questions and responses have shaped and developed my thinking.

I'm particularly indebted to the acting students of the Communal and Devised Theatre course at the Royal Central School of Speech and Drama for their enthusiasm and skill, and also to Catherine Alexander for her encouragement and support for my work.

To hire the masks featured in the book, please contact:
www.thewrightschool.co.uk

Half-masks and Naïve masks can be purchased from Mike Chase:
www.mikechasemasks.com

1
Raking Over a Few Gurus

There was once a great guru who everyone thought knew the secret to a happy life.

'Do you know what I'm going to teach you today?' he said.

'Yes,' said his followers.

'If you know that, then you have no use for me here.'

And he left, and went away.

Seven years later, the guru returned.

'Do you know what I'm going to teach you today?' he asked his followers.

'No,' they said. 'We know nothing.'

'If you know nothing,' said the guru, 'then you have no use for me here.'

And he left, and went away.

Seven years later, the guru returned.

'Do you know what I'm going to teach you today?' he said.

'Some of us do, and some of us don't,' they replied.

'Excellent,' he said. 'Then let those who think they know tell those who think they don't. You have no use for me here.'

And with that he left, and went away.

I'm reminded of this story whenever I think about the history of modern acting. Only last year, during a workshop in London, a student told me: 'You can't start Neutral Mask like that. You haven't done "the fundamental journey".' I politely told her that I wasn't interested in doing 'the fundamental journey'. What I really wanted to tell her, of course, was that I was far more likely to sing 'Abide With Me' to the tune of 'We Will Rock You' than do 'the fundamental journey'. What starts with a prophet invariably ends with a policeman. The Stanislavsky police have been around for years, but the Lecoq police are a new and very sad development. The irony is that, on the occasion of the thirtieth anniversary of his school in Paris, Lecoq put up a huge banner across the school courtyard declaring, 'Don't do what I do. Do what you do.' But it takes real bottle to find your way entirely on your own. We all need our 'gurus'. The world is a lonely place without them. Some gurus, we're told, simply give you 'permission' to be you. But when it comes to the teaching of acting, most gurus give us a 'process'; and the more you teach that process, the more that process is analysed; and the more it's reconstructed and taught again, the more it becomes codified into 'doing the fundamental journey'.

I admire the guru in the story. I admire his apparent lack of interest in having any disciples at all. He seems preoccupied with being somewhere else entirely. I even wonder if he really *is* a guru. He could just as easily have been a commercial traveller, doing a bit of 'guruing' on the side. But the brutal economy of his teaching is astonishing. He doesn't appear to do any, which is, of course, the whole point of the story: 'Let those who think they know tell those who think they don't.' I like the notion that it's all speculation, and that some of us are simply deceiving ourselves. Because, deep down, we do in fact *know*, and if we're really honest with ourselves, we've *known* all along. We simply like the idea of being taught what we already know, because we don't trust our own instincts. We can only teach *ourselves* how to have a happy life. All the guru can do is dismantle the barriers that stop us doing what we want to do. You're a waste of time if you think you know nothing at all, and if you think you know absolutely everything, then you're an even bigger waste of time. Only continual enquiry is encouraged: 'Let those who think they know tell those who think they don't.'

Problems arise the moment you become convinced of your own certainty, because that's when enquiry stops. Questions fade away once you think you *know*, and any idea that contradicts the chosen one looks faintly ridiculous. The notion that there's a one-size-fits-all system of acting is preposterous. The genius of Stanislavsky lay in the fact that his curiosity vastly outweighed his ego. His greatest gift was his ability to change his mind. He never stopped asking questions, and his work was continually evolving, and ultimately never finished. The story goes that, on meeting an actress whom he'd directed years before, she told him that she had pages of detailed notes of all the processes they'd explored together. 'What shall I do with them?' she asked. 'Burn them,' he replied. He was only interested in what was happening now, and nothing was fixed for long.

Sadly, there's no *right way* of teaching acting. In fact, I'm not convinced that you can teach anybody to do anything, other than the bare mechanics of an activity. You can learn to drive, for example. That's to say, you can be taught how to manage the controls of a car, but 'road-sense' is more of an empirical skill, and that's something you can only teach yourself. The best we can do in teaching any practical endeavour, beyond basic mechanical processes, is to enable each other to teach ourselves. And we do this by keeping the questions alive by continually making new proposals, rather than laying down rules. To quote the actor Edward Petherbridge, in his book *Slim Chances* (Indepenpress, 2011): 'I have always said that we can only be taught that which we already intrinsically know and are.' In other words, we can only use that which is a part of us. In acting, *you* are far more interesting and far more original than anything you can be taught, and in a culture of actor training that's dominated by other people's process, that's a vital observation.

The scene has changed in the UK over recent years, and the names of inspiring teachers are banded about like so many designer labels. Where you were once most likely to be asked, 'Where did you train?' the answer you're more likely to hear now is the name of the guru: 'I'm studying Meisner now' – as if everything else that's been done before is suddenly irrelevant. This Pentecostal approach to acting is, thankfully, not as strong in the UK as it is in the States, but it's definitely in the air. At its best, our culture of actor training is more pragmatic, although even here, actor training remains one of the most conservative areas in all the arts, because it's dominated by people *who know* rather than those who pose questions, and provoke us to find things out for ourselves.

The guru in the story refuses to tell his followers anything. In the end, he just congratulates them and walks away, leaving them to work things out for themselves. But I don't think he's a charlatan. It isn't that he won't tell them what to do because he can't be bothered. I think it's a preconceived teaching strategy: a game. He's showing his followers that to claim to know everything is just as pointless as claiming to know nothing at all. Certainty only makes us doctrinaire, but faux-naïvety is fundamentally dishonest. You can't pretend that you don't know anything. The irony is, of course, that the more the guru compels his followers to make up their own minds, the more they're all left thinking how wise he is.

Teachers who 'know' want to teach us things, while teachers who want us to teach ourselves refuse to disclose what they know. These teachers prefer to provoke us into coming to our own conclusions, in our different ways, rather than tell us what to do. We need our gurus because we want to know what they know, and to do what they do. And we need our gurus to 'know', and to be seen to 'know'. We want the certainty that we're doing things the right way, and the best way. It's fascinating to meet a teacher who clearly knows, but who at the same time also insists on concealing that precious knowledge. There's mystery and enigma here. But if you've got a teacher who isn't prepared to explain the difference between right and wrong, you'll be stuck thinking, 'How do we all move on?'

Rules

The best thing about the guru story is that, in just a few sentences, it brings us to an entirely logical conclusion, but we're not entirely sure whether the conclusion of the story is a profound enlightenment or a cynical manipulation. That question is left hanging in the air. Personally, I don't see any bullshit in this story. Even if we see it as a pre-planned teaching strategy, there are no lies or exaggerated nonsense here. When the guru walks away, he leaves his followers with nothing but their native wit and eager imagination. The trouble is, we all want rules, even if we know we're only going to break them in the end. We all want to be told what to do. Rules give us confidence; rules make us feel safe; but they also provoke us and give us something to kick against. Deep down inside, we all want to be good. And we all want to be seen to be good, and to be able to repeat that goodness and to measure it, so that we can show each other exactly how good we are. If only art was that simple and that organised! Because in art there's no right and wrong.

During a recent Q-and-A session at the British Museum, the potter Grayson Perry was warmly congratulated on his new exhibition by an elderly lady in the audience who marvelled at his imaginative vision, but complained that she feared for the creative vision of future generations of artists because her granddaughter 'only likes things in bright pink'. To which the artist replied: 'At least she's got rules.' Rules are invariably the first thing we look for in learning anything. We've all been taught to assess our learning by our ability to accurately follow the rules. Rules are our means of maintaining control in all aspects of our lives: law and order, health and safety, aesthetic convention, style, political conviction, personal taste, power in all its forms – all these are the direct consequences of our love affair with rules.

Love them or hate them, we can't do without them. And anarchy won't get you anywhere. Remove the rules and you create a vacuum. There'll always be rules, and you can't take one set away without finding yourself immediately imposing another. I'm wary of rules, but if you read between the lines you'll find this book is full of them. Rules are intrinsic to the way we learn and interpret the world around us. In theatre, rules shape our conventions and compel us to make choices. Rules shape the way we interact on stage, and they're essential in enabling us to repeat and recreate what we've made in the past.

The trouble is, the more we theorise, and examine rules in the abstract, the more conceptual the work becomes, and so we end up thinking more about the ideas behind what we're doing than processing the experience of the work itself. We're told that the theory informs the practice but in reality it's the other way round: the practice informs the theory. Empiricism and personal discovery vastly outweigh theoretical speculation.

The Way We Learn

Neuromuscular activities, like standing, walking, running, jumping, catching a ball, as well as almost everything we refer to as body language and non-verbal communication, are all learned instinctively. We learn them through an innate process of trial and error. This is learning based on unconscious discoveries, on feelings and sensations that we're totally unaware of, rather than on carefully considered thoughts and ideas. Rules don't come in to this process. Of course, with the benefit of hindsight, we can reduce and summarise anything down to a series of rules. In infancy, for example, we might have taught ourselves in our own way how to stand up, and walk about. But if you had to teach someone else how to stand up and walk about, you'd soon find yourself articulating a very precise set of rules to make that activity happen.

Neurologists tell us that instinctive learning and personal discovery engage the brain in an entirely different way from learning derived from the conscious application of a clear set of instructions. I don't know any actors who work in the way they were taught at drama school, and some of the most exciting actors I've ever worked with didn't go to drama school at all. After only a year or so in the business, most of us find our own way of doing things. The training might influence us, but we won't be dominated by it for ever. Our deepest learning comes through trial and error: watching each other, following our enthusiasms and trying things out for ourselves.

The Dreyfus Brothers

In the 1970s, two psychologists, known as the Dreyfus brothers, did some interesting research into how we acquire skills. Much to my delight, they came to the conclusion that the empirical 'suck it and see' approach to learning that compels you to discover things for yourself is ultimately more rewarding, and more valuable, than the conventional method whereby you're actively taught the 'right way' or the 'approved way' of doing something. Their work trashed the mantra that 'practice makes perfect', and proposed instead that learning through personal experience is deeper, more flexible, and ultimately more effective in its application than the conventional model of learning an approved routine. Hardly earth-shattering, you might think. Edward Petherbridge and Grayson Perry would probably give this idea their full approval, but I wonder how many acting teachers would buy in to it? After all, if you're devoted to a particular system – if you've studied the Method in detail, for example – you'll probably think you've got a season ticket to the promised land already.

The Dreyfus brothers identified five stages in the acquisition of skill:

1. The **novice**, who adheres to the rules, with no discretionary judgement.

2. The **beginner**, who feels compelled to adhere to the rules, and who only has a tiny range of personal experience to draw on.

3. The **competent person**, who has studied, arranged and organised the rules into a personal routine that they can cope with more easily.

4. The **proficient person**, who's the one with enough experience to disregard all rules and procedures, and tends to work from maxims, but can't resist subverting the rules at the same time.

5. The **expert**, who's abandoned all rules, all procedures and all maxims, and who works entirely from intuition.

When you read that list, self-assessment is irresistible. We all want to know our positions on it. The difference between the **novice** and the **expert** is that the **novice** has no personal experience to draw on, whereas the **expert** has learned and absorbed all the rules and played with them, and broken them, in so many different ways that rules are, at best, little more than a point of departure. For the **expert**, personal instinct is far more important than conventional procedure. Rules and established processes are only returned to in novel circumstances, or if something goes wrong. This research isn't an argument against rules and systematic learning, but rather an examination of our long-term attitude towards rules and, by implication, how we teach ourselves.

Lenard Petit, an inspiring teacher of the 'Michael Chekhov technique', told me recently that he kept returning to that practice because, more than anything else, it gave him personal freedom. I've heard other people say much the same about actor-training systems – and that's all well and good. The big lesson to take away from the Dreyfus brothers' five stages of learning is that no matter who your guru is, personal freedom and personal empowerment is the ultimate goal in the acquisition of skill. But if you want to be an **expert**, there comes a point where you've simply got to chuck the satnav out of the window and find your own way.

Personal freedom transcends methods, systems and techniques, because it starts from *you*. The great teacher Dorothy Heathcote used to tell her students to 'assume the mantle of the expert'. There's no apparent system to instinctive learning. There's no method or particular technique. It instantly confronts you with yourself, and gives you space to enable you to become aware of what you're doing. Systems, methods and techniques, however well they work, are always someone else's big idea. **Experts** transcend other people's 'big ideas' by making choices based on empirical understanding. In other words, they've tried it one way, didn't like it much, so they've found another that they liked a lot better. It sounds simplistic, but ultimately that's what happens: **experts** trust their own observations and their own impulses over principles and processes laid down by other people.

Expertise is an instinctive process of personal discovery, like the neuromuscular learning of the intrepid toddler. Your initial training as an actor might have mapped out the territory, and enabled you to plan your journey up the mountain by an established route, but the **expert** prefers to go off-piste: not necessarily as an act of rebellion, but more from the desire to walk unaided. To return to the driving analogy: you can learn the Highway Code by rote, but how you read the road, and how you react to the prevailing conditions, is ultimately something you find for yourself. Within a few months of driving on your own, you develop your own style and that initial instruction soon becomes a thing of the past. Acting is much the same.

In Dreyfus terminology, the **expert** is someone whose skills have been honed through personal discovery and revelation. In other words, they've driven through the centre of town, in the rush hour, innumerable times, on their own. They know where the danger spots are; they know what they have to do and what they prefer to do; and they're sufficiently knowledgeable about all these things to take their own risks. It's knowledge that can only grow and develop if you think for yourself and follow your instincts. The liberating element here is the loss of that deadly obligation to 'get it right' according to someone else's standards. Suddenly all those well-established 'shoulds' and essential processes are put under review. Now, nothing is set in stone, and personal reactions are more important than anything you've been told to believe. But systems, methods and techniques don't make the journey from **novice** to **expert** any easier. Those first three stages on the Dreyfus scale, from the **novice** to the **competent person**, invariably leave an indelible mark on the psyche.

Big-Boy Stan

Stanislavsky is by far the most seminal acting teacher of all. He devoted his life to perfecting 'the definitive system of acting', and I can't write the name 'Stanislavsky' without the musty smell of dogmatism oozing off the page. The more seminal the teacher, it would seem, the more disciples they have toiling away to keep the work going – but in reality, working even harder to keep it exactly the same. When this happens, systems turn into dogmas, and ideas become codified into conventional routines. But the most crippling thing of all happens when speculation turns into certainty. However, we love certainty. Certainty gives us confidence. Unfortunately, certainty also breeds complacency, and complacency kills exploration and the emergence of new ideas. The faintest whiff of absolute truth stifles enquiry.

The word 'truth' is traditionally associated with acting, but 'truth' is as joyless as religious fundamentalism, and just as confrontational. 'I'm only interested in truthful acting. Pretence is for children,' a pompous American acting teacher once told me during a session at the International Workshop Festival, some time in the eighties. Vintage bullshit, I'm afraid. But the paradoxical idea that the best acting must be 'truthful' has preoccupied academics for decades, and left us all with an obsession with verisimilitude, and with the heartfelt belief that being lifelike is the same as being 'truthful'. The concept has been given added credibility by being attributed to Stan the Man himself, but it's worth noting that the idea that good acting must be 'truthful' was originally conceived simply to sell his books. According to Jean Benedetti, in *An Actor's Work* (Routledge, 2008), the term 'truthful acting' was invented by Stanislavsky's American translator and editor, Elizabeth Hapgood.

Stanislavsky was hugely inspired by the newly emerging science of 'psychology', and the idea of creating psychological realism on stage was the driving force behind his work at that point. Hapgood knew that this would sell on the American market, but Stanislavsky always tried to use 'homely language' in his writing, as part of a determined effort to suppress jargon. But Hapgood wanted to make his work look more profound, so she invented a jargon of her own. Stanislavsky never talked about acting being 'truthful', for example. He talked about effective acting as being 'alive'. Similarly, he talked about 'tasks' rather than 'objectives', 'thoughts' rather than 'inner monologues', and 'bits' rather than 'units' or 'beats', as they tend to be called today. (I've never understood what people mean by 'beats'.) He described how it was possible to cut a scene up into different chunks, and arrange them, in sequence, to see how they all fitted together – rather like a butcher jointing a piece of meat.

In America, Big-Boy Stan inspired innumerable imitators: a veritable host of gurus, each with a slightly different take on the original teaching of the great man. These were the Method-mongers, each with their own 'take' on the original teaching: such names as Sanford Meisner, Stella Adler, Lee Strasberg and Uta Hagen, and more recently, in England, Mike Alfreds, Bella Merlin and Dee Cannon. 'Social realism' may have replaced 'psychological realism', but Stan the Man's influence is as potent today as it ever was. To the vast majority of us, he's still 'top guru'. He's still the one who 'really knows'. But in France, another smaller, and more enigmatic, group of gurus emerged at the start of the last century, who differed radically from the Stanislavskians in both what they taught and how they taught it. These teachers didn't have a system, refused to tell us what to do, and insisted that you find your own solutions for yourself. No surprises there then. And their arch-guru was Jacques Copeau.

Copeau and the Mask

If the impact of psychological realism struck darkly resonant chords in our understanding of acting, the role of masks in the way we train our actors remains a distant, and almost inaudible, echo. If Stanislavsky laid the foundations of the way we look at acting, Jacques Copeau laid the foundations of our understanding of how masks work, and how we might use masks in theatre training. But, more significantly, he also set down a few markers as to how acting might be taught. While Stanislavsky was getting his students to explore their emotional memories, Copeau's students were trying to capture the movement of birds and animals. While Stanislavsky was wrestling with naturalism and the uncompromising determination to be lifelike, Copeau was preoccupied with style – exploring ways of representing reality through metaphor and irony, through graceful economy or grotesque exaggeration. Where Stanislavsky would add multiple layers of psychological realism, Copeau was busy stripping all the psychology away.

The 'Ten Commandments'

Stanislavsky's basic teaching has become common currency in most of our drama schools. He analysed and articulated what he thought acting was all about, wrestling with the problems of appearing to be credible in fictional circumstances. In his hands, acting became logical, rational and intelligent. The idea of having 'one [system] to rule them all' became a tantalising prospect after the American publication of *An Actor Prepares* in 1936, and it contributed greatly to the Dreyfus model of learning gaining a strong foothold in our drama schools. Stalwart Stanislavskians have taken generations of drama students from the **novice** to the **proficient person**. How many of them can boast the accolade of spawning **experts** I don't know.

Take a look at this. I've taken this extract from an article in a special supplement on acting and performing that appeared in the *Guardian* on the work of Dee Cannon. Here she sets down an important part of her approach to acting, drawing on what Stanislavsky called 'the given circumstances':

> This is based around Stanislavsky's acting technique, and his seven key questions which, over the years, I have adapted into ten key acting questions every actor should answer in order to be a fully rounded and connected actor.
>
> 1. *Who am I?*
>
> 2. *Where am I?*
>
> 3. *When is it?*
>
> 4. *Where have I just come from?*
>
> 5. *What do I want?*
>
> 6. *Why do I want it?*
>
> 7. *Why do I want it now?*
>
> 8. *What will happen if I don't get it now?*
>
> 9. *What do I have to do to get what I want?*
>
> 10. *What must I overcome?*

Ten answers to be found; ten things to remember; ten 'shoulds'; ten rules of interpretation; 'Ten Commandments'. They make us feel secure and confident in the knowledge that we're in control and that we know exactly what we're doing. And what could possibly be wrong with that? You might think the short answer is 'Nothing' – provided you don't believe that answering all these questions is the only responsible way of making theatre. Conventional wisdom tells us that Dee Cannon's 'Ten Commandments' are an intelligent set of choices that will eventually enable you to 'become the character'. Almost all the actor training in the Western world is based on work like this, and it's immensely useful. It's probably the first thing I'd turn to if I were reading an obscure or complicated scene. But these rules are a world away from the sheer delight of throwing a shoe on the floor as hard as you can, just to make your friends jump.

The 'Ten Commandments' make complete sense and give us all the information we need to be (as Dee Cannon might say) a 'fully rounded' and 'connected' actor – but are these attributes absolutely vital on all occasions? They make a hopeless devising strategy, for example, and they'd make playing masks impossible because they're more interpretive than provocative. They deal with circumstances that a good playwright will already have put in place. They're a set of questions designed to enable you to connect with a dramatic situation that's already written and firmly placed in the 'there-and-then', rather than compelling you to make your own choices and your own provocations in the 'here-and-now'. And do you always need to be that connected? Isn't it occasionally a good idea simply to be 'dropped in it', and to be deliberately 'put in the shit'? Genuinely not knowing, and genuinely not understanding, are potentially powerful and profound impulses to play.

Directors like Alfred Hitchcock, for example, thought nothing of putting his actors into deeply uncomfortable, not to say dangerous, situations in order to get the right shot. The director Mike Leigh is likewise renowned for establishing situations where the actors are given no alternative *but* to be in the here-and-now. When the police came to arrest Imelda Staunton as Vera Drake, in the film of the same name, she genuinely had no idea what was happening, and the event took her completely by surprise. In fact, the police arrived in the middle of the family's Sunday lunch. I doubt that any careful study of the 'Ten Commandments' helped her then. When you genuinely don't know, then all you can do is 'let it happen' and follow your instincts. And a brilliant performance was the result.

It's hardly surprising that so much acting training leaves you with a grim determination to 'get it right'. It feels more assertive; you appear to be working with 'rigour' when you have something to achieve. Being prepared to simply 'let it happen' sounds unintelligent and irresponsible. The Dreyfus model of learning, at least up to the level of the **proficient person**, assures you that if you can 'get it right', then you know what you're doing. But *play* has nothing to do with knowledge, and precious little to do with conscious understanding of any kind. It's more about personal reactions than accurate interpretation and, as such, it's a distinctly hit-and-miss affair: you might be good now, but if you don't know what you're doing, how will you ever repeat it?

But it's 'unreliable', we're told. 'You work quicker, and with more confidence, when you know what you're doing.' As the director of the International School of Screen Acting once told me: 'In an industry where time is money, who would you put your money on: the guy who's just going to have a go, or the person who's worked it all out beforehand?' But I can't answer that question until I know the person who's up for 'having a go'. If I trust that person, I'd let them 'have a go' every time, because I know I'd find it more exciting.

In making the astonishingly popular Danish TV series *The Killing* (2007), the actors were only given the script one episode at time. None of the actors involved knew who the killer was until the last possible moment. The effect was to fix our attention on every little detail. The body language was dripping with ambiguity and dramatic tension, and because we didn't know whom we could trust, every turn of events became an open question, and the acting was correspondingly compelling to watch. It's another example of instinctive reactions having more weight and complexity than actions that are preconceived.

Moshe Feldenkrais

The movement teacher Moshe Feldenkrais was a famous nuclear physicist, the first Caucasian judo black belt, and a seminal teacher of the way we learn through movement. Like Edward Petherbridge and the Dreyfus brothers, Feldenkrais maintained that we find the deepest and most creative learning for ourselves. He first came into prominence in the theatre world about forty years ago, through his work with Peter Brook, who invited him to work with his company at Bouffes du Nord in Paris, in the seventies.

Brook was at that time exploring a range of fundamental questions that were designed to take nothing for granted about our understanding of theatre, what it is and what it does. Questions such as: What is simplicity? What is fantasy? When does walking turn into dancing? Can actors create? Does creation happen by itself? What's the relationship between the abstract and the real? Brook was sure that Feldenkrais could take them straight to the essence of how we learn, and for Brook, this went straight to the heart of the work.

Feldenkrais structured his teaching into what he called 'Awareness Through Movement' lessons that focused his teaching on tiny physical detail and made it very personal. There was no comparison between one individual and another, and certainly no universal standard to live up to. For Feldenkrais, the journey was more important than the arrival. In other words, he believed that we learn more from what we find on the way, in the form of little personal discoveries, than we ever do from a battle-scarred, dogged determination to 'get there' or to 'get it right'. He'd tell you that there was a hidden agenda behind each movement, but it was up to you to find out what that was. There was no 'right' and 'wrong' for Feldenkrais: there were only differences. 'Differences are interesting, differences are creative,' he used to say. His work was more about personal play, and personal discovery, than any achievement that we might all recognise. But it's the way he conducted his teaching that fascinates me.

Feldenkrais would never tell you why you were doing any particular movement, or where it was all leading. And that notion of *not knowing* is essential to the theme of personal exploration and discovery. If you don't know why you're doing something, your instinct to achieve is seriously compromised. It's a direct invitation to do a movement purely for its own sake, just to see what it feels like.

An 'Awareness Through Movement' lesson could start from anywhere. It could be something as simple as sitting down, and moving your right shoulder and your head together in order to touch your cheek several times, and then *resting*. Then resuming the shoulder movement again and exploring the extent you can touch your shoulder with your chin, touch your shoulder with your ear, or perhaps slide your cheek against your shoulder from the ear to the chin. Variations like these keep us interested and entertained, but enthusiasm can easily slip into achievement.

This is where the 'rests' come in. These 'rests' are surprising, at first. After all, why rest when you've barely done anything? But the rests are another way of emphasising that you don't know why you're doing this movement. And it's in the rests where the work really starts, because you're not doing this to get fitter or to lose weight. It won't improve your cardiovascular fitness. The rests give you the space and time to feel the consequences of the movement. This is where you can 'listen in' to what your shoulder feels like. And then start again.

The little variations on what it feels like to move the chin to the shoulder, as opposed to moving the ear to the shoulder, are an invitation to turn the movement into a game. Games are fun. Games are entertaining because their only function is to give pleasure and to keep that pleasure alive. And as long as the movement doesn't hurt, and you don't find yourself straining to go further, 'finding the game' gives you more to 'suck and see' when you've finished the movement. At the end of the sequence, when you stand up for that final 'rest', you can feel the difference between the right shoulder and the left. The feeling of ease and space in the right side of your neck, together with the fact that your right arm hangs in a different way than it did before and now seems to be half an inch longer, is fascinating.

This is a tiny fragment of a Feldenkrais lesson, but it illustrates my point. He might have called it a 'lesson', but I call it a 'game'. Scientists would call it a 'proprioceptive game': in other words, a game to make you more aware of your own body, how you move and how you hold yourself. Feldenkrais was trying to inspire learning from the place where everything starts – namely, in the body. It's an approach to learning based on the exploration of the physical movements of babies. After all, rolling over, standing up and learning to walk are the greatest physical achievements that the vast majority of us will ever experience.

The change of feeling at the end of that brief shoulder sequence is remarkable. But Feldenkrais wasn't employed purely for actor maintenance; he was more than Peter Brook's resident physio. Feldenkrais was there because his work was as much about play, exploration and creativity as it was about posture and economy. Which is a surprising conclusion to come from a respected scientist with a black belt in judo. The story goes that he suffered a serious knee injury and doctors told him that he'd never walk again without a stick, but his continual physical exploration proved them wrong and he went on to evolve a means of investigating how we learn.

I don't think Feldenkrais would have been particularly interested in the Dreyfus model of learning. For all that it encourages you to look at the way you apply certain aspects of a received body of knowledge, in an 'Awareness Through Movement' lesson the last thing you need to know is your position on an ascending scale of expertise, especially when you're letting things go their own way with nothing to achieve in the first place.

But Feldenkrais never completely turned his back on the scientific world. His early work with nuclear physics had given him some prestige, and he lectured at CERN, the European organisation for nuclear research, had many high-level neuroscientists as friends, and was exceptionally well read in all the new discoveries. He even followed his wife's paediatric studies, en route to her becoming a doctor, but when people asked why he never obtained a medical qualification himself, he said that, if he had, he would have had to believe everything the clever doctors said; in which case he would never have been able to discover what he did.

In the Beginning was the Mask…

Feldenkrais doesn't stand alone, however, in dashing the myth of the expert and casting 'you' in that role right from the start. Jacques Copeau made no attempt to put on record his ideas on actor training that he'd developed at his school in Burgundy. He discovered that his students embraced his ideas more effectively when left to play with them on their own. Rather than leading from the front, Copeau developed a style of teaching that enabled his students to evolve ideas for themselves, and he'd let their preoccupations shape the curriculum. In the long run he found it more exciting to play along with them rather than tell them what to do. In that way they were all involved in the same process of discovery.

The Handkerchief Game

The story goes that Copeau was once confronted with a young actor who was so consumed with self-consciousness that she found it impossible to keep still. In a final act of desperation, he draped a handkerchief over her entire face, like a veil. Apparently, this bizarre initiative immediately made her feel incognito and therefore more comfortable in herself, which enabled her to stop fidgeting, stay still, and to engage more directly with the experience of being on stage: a bit like covering a budgie's cage in order to send it to sleep. The success with the handkerchief, so we're told, gave Copeau the idea of using masks to train actors, which in turn led him to reconsider his entire approach to acting and theatre-making, and to start a tradition of actor training based on instinctive play inspired by mask-work.

In the 1950s, Copeau's nephew, Michel Saint-Denis, brought these ideas about using masks in training actors over to England. At this time the movers and shakers of British theatre were hungry for new ideas and Saint-Denis was able to work alongside the best of them. At the Royal Court, he worked closely with George Devine, who passed these new ideas on to Keith Johnstone, whose book *Impro* has had a seminal influence on our training and theatre-making in England to this day. In France, Jean Dorcy, a former student of Copeau, passed his version of Copeau's teaching on to the young Jacques Lecoq, who in turn passed it on to Philippe Gaulier and Monika Pagneux. They're all very different teachers, but they all use masks to some extent in their work, and they all value play as a vital growth point in theatre-making.

The theory behind the Handkerchief Game is that covering her face gave this young girl something to hide behind. Once she was safe in the knowledge that so much of her face was hidden, she felt that her feelings were also hidden and she could relax and build a warmer relationship with the audience.

There are two ways of playing Copeau's Handkerchief Game. You can either drape the handkerchief to cover the entire face like a veil, or you can fold it diagonally in half and tie it over your nose and mouth, like a bank robber in an old cowboy film. The *veil* version of the game has the effect of putting up a tangible barrier between you and the audience. This barrier not only hides your features but it also restricts what you can do. It covers your eyes and obscures your vision, which inevitably slows you down, and compels you to focus your attention on where you are and what you're doing. On the outside, the veil is a complete covering and a constant reminder that this is a piece of material put in place to hide something, which makes you look more enigmatic. Under a veil you need no further confirmation that you're completely hidden, which gives you the space to interact with the people watching you.

The *bank-robber* version only covers half your face. On the inside you still feel anonymous and hidden, but you feel more in control than you do with the *veil* version because you can see exactly where you are, whilst being safe in the knowledge that we can't see the bottom half of your face. From the outside, there's less mystery in a face whose eyes we can see. We might not have a whole face to work with, but the eyes are clearly visible and informative. The trouble is that we don't necessarily believe what they're telling us because we can't see what your mouth is doing, and because we don't see why you've covered your face in this way in the first place. We like a face to give us the complete picture. From the outside you look more intriguing than enigmatic.

I've played both versions of the Handkerchief Game and found that it reflects something crucial about the way that masks work. My distinct preference is for the *veil* version because it has the strongest impact for all concerned. To have a piece of cloth draped over your face when you're nervous and self-conscious, or brimming over with adrenalin, will certainly inspire a complete change of feeling. The *veil* version of the game works more like a full-mask, namely a mask that covers the entire face. The *bank-robber* version, however, works more like a half-mask, where only half of the face is covered. From the outside, the *veil* has the effect of taking you out of the picture completely because we have no face with discernible features for us to relate to. We all know it's there, but we can't see it, and we can't read your intentions. The *bank-robber* version tends to be more fun because its more like an audacious joke. It personifies the lie that you can't see my whole face, but that it doesn't matter. It *does* matter. The more we don't believe you, the more you're impelled to mess about for the fun of it.

This is the game that gave Copeau the inspiration to use masks as a means of training actors and in doing so opened up a whole new raft of work that we're still reaping the benefits of today. (The only trouble is that so few of us carry freshly laundered handkerchiefs around with us these days. Paper tissues are simply not the same. I use scraps of material.)

The big lesson to be learned from the Handkerchief Game is the role of the eyes in mask-work.

The Spectacles Game

Bring the tips of your forefingers and the tips of your thumbs together to make two circles, like a bizarre pair of glasses. If you now lift them to your face, and look through the holes you've made, and then look at another person through your spectacles, you'll start to feel hidden. If you look closely at the person next to you, then suddenly remove your hands from your eyes, you'll immediately feel exposed. If you then look out from behind your hands, you'll get the stupid idea that you can't be seen, in spite of the fact that you could hardly make yourself more conspicuous.

This is the effect that the Handkerchief Game is referring to, but it doesn't work if you don't cover your eyes in some way. If you play the *bank-robber* version of the Handkerchief Game, and if you bring the top fold of the handkerchief so close to your eyes that you're aware of a dark line of the material just below your line of vision, you'll feel just as 'hidden' as you do from looking out from behind your hands. In the *veil* version of the game the facial covering is more complete. Your eyes disappear completely, to the point where your inability to see clearly becomes a useful restriction to play with. The big eyeholes created by the thumbs and forefingers in the Spectacles Game give you no perceivable restrictions at all, but your awareness of your fingers round your eyes, and the occasional dark shadows they create, give you the feeling of being hidden. But if you now curl your index fingers up against your thumbs in order to make a set of very small holes to look through – what we might call 'pinhole eyes' – you'll immediately see how visual restriction is a vital part of mask design.

If you want a mask that can move and react quickly, you need large eyeholes. But if you want the mask to move slowly and carefully, the smaller eyeholes will be more appropriate.

I've tried the Handkerchief Game for myself, in similar circumstances to those that Copeau was confronted with in the 1930s, when he originally invented the game. I was working at a drama school in North London, some time in the seventies, and I can assure you that the Handkerchief Game didn't work for me at all. I adopted exactly the same strategy as outlined in the Copeau story. I was working with a first-year drama student, consumed with self-consciousness, but the moment I covered her face with a cloth, the audience exploded into laughter, and she abruptly pulled it off and sat down again, feeling even worse than she had when she started. The group told me that she looked like a medium in a séance when I draped the cloth over her face, and concluded that the game was bizarre.

As a young visiting lecturer, close in age to my students, it was ridiculous of me to assume that I could possibly emulate a teaching strategy adopted by an eminent practitioner, at an entirely different time and in another country, and which I'd read about in a book. It wasn't the game that was at fault but my ineptitude as a teacher. But today, when I use a full-mask, with features that capture a recognisably human face, it has the same function as Copeau's handkerchief and it works every time.

Only a few months ago, in a workshop I run for potential members of the Actors Centre in London, I encountered an uncomfortable young actor high on adrenalin...

When I arrived at the space, the previous session had just finished, and I found the group sitting around chatting and playing some gentle relaxing music, off someone's phone, on the sound system. As I was setting out a set of masks on the table, I noticed a young woman dancing manically about, in a show of confidence that looked like someone who preferred to be busy. An earnest young man was apologising to me whilst trying to switch the music off.

'Do you have something better to dance to?' I asked him, and two or three people set about choosing some suitable tracks from their phones.

'There's so much to choose from,' said one of them.

Meanwhile I went over to our exhibitionist dancer and asked her if she wanted to play a game in a mask. She tentatively accepted my offer.

'Don't worry,' I told her. 'I won't leave you in the shit.' Then I turned her away from the audience and asked her to close her eyes whilst I put her in the mask.

(Personal Journal, 2014)

I'd chosen the mask of **The Victim**, but she knew nothing about that; in fact, the less she knew about it, the better. The workshop I was about to start was on 'Character' – What is it? Where does it come from? Do we make it? Is it found? Or is it something you have already? And the answers to all these questions were to be found in the playing a few masks.

I'd chosen **The Victim** because it struck me as a complete contrast to the qualities I'd seen in our dancer when I first came in the room.

The Victim: played by Rakhee Sharma

This is the face of a person who looks overcome with self-consciousness, and appears to be the epitome of low self-esteem and rejection. I'd chosen this mask because it personified entirely contrasting qualities to those I'd seen in our dancer when she was messing about to the music as I came in the room…

'But I won't be able to do anything with my eyes closed.'

'Don't worry, I'll help you,' I replied, 'and if it doesn't work, you can always blame me because that's what I'm paid for.'

The audience laughed, but I don't think she was convinced.

'On my cue, the orchestra will play and the artist will turn round, open her eyes and dance.'

I gave the signal, and bang on cue, raunchy rock and roll boomed out of the speakers, our dancer turned round and danced across the space, and the audience erupted into laughter as soon as they saw the mask. But, watching from the side, I could see that more and more people were starting to copy the face of the mask. They were all pulling the same face.

'Yes, she's funny,' they were thinking 'but that face was anything but funny.'

Behind the mask, our dancer didn't know what was happening and she stopped in her tracks. She was clearly startled by the effect she was having on us. A few minutes ago she'd been dancing about, oblivious of everyone around her, but now at the centre of attention, our reactions to her had shocked her to the core.

'Change the music,' I commanded, and rhapsodic classical music came out of the speakers. Our dancer looked confused, but assumed a balletic pose. The audience roared with laughter again. The clash between what she was doing and what she looked like was incongruous. Now her dance became even more 'balletic'. She knew what was happening now, and she was starting to play, which ironically made the mask look all the more out of place, and we all erupted into sustained laughter as she leapt about the space with a face that looked utterly appalled with everything. At the peak of the laughter I stopped the scene, and she took the mask off to thunderous applause, then looked, in total disbelief, at the pained-looking face she'd just delighted us all with.

That young actor didn't know what she was doing and she didn't know why she was doing it, but my point is that she didn't need to know. It would have taken far too long to explain how acting works in a mask like this, and I'm not convinced that any of that information would have helped her play any better. As it was, she found a persona, and a personal pleasure, in what she was doing – all by herself. In the best Copeau tradition she was beginning to become her own **expert**.

The problem with mask-work and the Dreyfus model of learning is that you can't take a mask home and play it in the privacy of your own front room, because mask-work only comes alive when you have an audience to play to. Mask-work is learning in the here-and-now: from what you do and how we react to seeing you do it. The Dreyfus model of learning is mostly in the there-and-then. You only start to move on to the here-and-now learning at the very end: once you hit the level of the **expert**. At that stage the Dreyfus model serves you very well. But Edward

Petherbridge's statement that 'we can only be taught that which we already intrinsically know and are' is still ringing in my ears.

It was the immediacy with which that uncomfortable young actor danced the **Victim Mask** that compelled her to draw her own conclusions and to teach herself. Edward Petherbridge's statement could hardly have been more prescient at this point. Acting is primarily about *you* and your reaction to events and stimuli: you're the **expert** here. Whether your guru is Strasberg, Stanislavsky, Michael Chekhov, Sanford Meisner, Jacques Copeau, Jacques Lecoq, Mike Alfreds, Bella Merlin, Dee Cannon or Philippe Gaulier, it doesn't matter. You've got to teach yourself in the end.

The Dreyfus model is about you learning to manage someone else's ideas, someone else's theories and someone else's processes. You're dealing with work that has been explained and demonstrated to you beforehand. But when you 'assume the mantle of the expert', as Dorothy Heathcote advised her young students, you must leave your guru behind and start to work things out for yourself. 'Don't do what I do. Do what you do,' Lecoq told us. Over the years my empathy has grown for a bewildered, slightly overweight, red-faced young actor I once saw at a Gaulier clown workshop. He was wearing an ill-fitting Viking costume at the time, and he'd been acting his socks off for the past five minutes. '*You* are more interesting than anything you can make up,' Gaulier had told him.

Behind a mask (be it a piece of cloth draped over your entire face like a veil, a beautifully sculptured representation of someone who feels deeply wronged, or an ill-fitting Viking costume), you're not playing with an idea – you're reacting to things happening in the here-and-now. This is theatre on legs. You put the mask on, turn round, look at the audience, and we all react. Behind the mask you can see us, hear us, and watch us all reacting, and you can't help yourself reacting to what you see and hear. Whether it makes you want to calm us down, cheer us up, or simply shock us even further, your honesty will make your choices as credible as they can get, because to all intents and purposes they're real.

The Tomato-Sandwich Incident

It was in the late sixties. I was a first-year drama student in a Christmas show touring a few primary schools in North London. We'd arrived early at this particular school. We needed a mirror, and one of the teachers directed me to a classroom to get one…

Entering that classroom was like landing on Mars. All around me there were children wearing huge colourful papier mâché heads that had been made on big balloons. Their chins, mouths, noses and eyes had been added later. I could see a few of them drying round the room, in various stages of construction. Small groups of children seemed to be rehearsing scenes. I couldn't see the teacher anywhere. But there was a Lollipop Lady, ushering imaginary children across an imaginary road, and two little boys in vast Teddy boy masks, with huge quiffs and sideburns. I watched them suddenly run into a corner, crumple bits of newspaper, and stuff it under their pullovers to make padded shoulders. Then they looked ridiculously pleased with themselves, slumped against the wall, trying to look menacing. They were like grotesque comic actors from ancient Rome.

Their teacher, in his paint-spattered overall, was preoccupied and harassed. He was struggling to glue an elaborate yellow paper wig, or rather lots of little bits of curly yellow paper, on to the head of a mask that was clearly the property of a nervous little girl, who stood near by, looking on, like an anxious relative in a hospital.

'The mirror's over there,' the teacher told me absent-mindedly, barely looking up from what he was doing. 'You can take it away. Once they've finished with it.'

Blocking my way, in front of the mirror, sat a little girl in the mask of an Old Woman with a smiley face. Her white curly-paper hair was forcing its way out from under an old felt hat. The Old Woman (or was it the little girl just being herself? I wasn't sure) was sitting with her back to the mirror rooting about in a school bag.

And this is what fascinated me: I couldn't tell if what she was doing was for real, or if she was acting. She was so completely credible. Eventually she produced a gym shoe, and handed it to the most angry-looking woman you could imagine. She had bushy black eyebrows, knitted together in an expression of perpetual fury. Her mouth was twisted into a shape that could have easily been a fist. Her thick black paper hair was squashed under a colourful headscarf, which was tied in a bow under her jutting paper chin. She took the gym shoe from the Old Woman and threw it on the floor in front of her with a loud slap. The whole room seemed to stop what it was doing at that point, but the teacher just continued with his glueing.

The Angry Woman was looking at a little girl, who was half the size of her, limping about the space, wearing a solitary gym shoe. She had a recalcitrant look on her face, and spiky black hair sticking bolt upright, as if she'd recently had an electric shock. She was a sort of female version of Dennis the Menace, except that she appeared to be trembling. Her arms and shoulders were shaking. In spite of this, she made herself stride past the Angry Woman, who seemed to be her mum, and over to the Old Woman. Then she grabbed the school bag from off the Old Woman's lap and emptied its contents on the floor in front of her.

I thought Angry Mum was going to explode. She stood, stock-still, her chest heaving up and down. Suddenly the Old Woman leapt to her feet and moved towards the Wayward Schoolgirl as if to protect her, and the Wayward Schoolgirl was trembling even more now. But when I looked at the Old Woman, what I originally took to be a smiley face now looked as if it was about to burst into tears. She was pointing at the mess of things on the floor, and my attention was drawn to a slightly squashed tomato sandwich as it rolled out of its thick greaseproof paper wrapping – and exposed itself in front of everyone. We all laughed. The spell was broken. Angry Mum took her mask off to reveal a big, round, slightly red face that immediately exploded into laughter. The Old Lady turned out to be a little girl with long blonde hair trying to rescue her lunch, and when the Wayward Schoolgirl took her mask off, I could see that she was giggling uncontrollably. 'Is that why she looked so terrified?' I asked myself.

'I think you've finished with the mirror now, haven't you, girls?' the teacher said now, from behind his pile of cut-up curly bits of yellow paper. At which point I took the opportunity to wheel the mirror past them, and out of the room.

(Personal Journal, 1969)

I'd never seen anything like this. The masks were preposterously exaggerated, and at the same time, so real. This was comic-strip reality. Those huge round heads with their paper hair and crudely formed, painted features have stuck in my mind ever since. They weren't lifelike, but they were instantly recognisable. Clearly, they were two-dimensional caricatures – they weren't remotely subtle – but I knew exactly who they were from the moment I saw them. They were 'types', yet either by accident or design, they seemed to go beyond type to reveal something more human and more vulnerable.

I also remember being astonished by the fact that, even though those masks had distorted features, once I'd recognised the type of person they were supposed to be, the fact that such a face was an anatomical impossibility didn't bother me in the slightest. I accepted each mask for what it was, and got on with watching the action. But their teacher wasn't watching. He was far too busy with that yellow hair. I got the feeling that he'd probably made all the masks himself, and the children had simply 'helped'. But that didn't matter. I don't think they were doing an art lesson. They all seemed far more intent on using the masks rather than making them.

It was their acting that astonished me: it was so subtle, so effortless and economical. For the most part, I could barely tell if they were acting at all. Time plays tricks on memory, but I remember being fascinated by the fact that they were just as credible when they were sorting things out amongst themselves as when they were actually playing their scene. They'd stop, stock-still, in the middle of something, and start talking to each other, and then immediately return to 'the acting', and you could hardly tell the difference. I remember thinking then that what they were doing in their classroom could hardly have been more different from what we were doing in our show. We were always so careful to make sure that everybody saw our 'acting'.

Compared to them, we were so serious. We were so obsessed with how we should be doing something that the gap for us between the thinking and the doing was enormous. 'Children's play is artless,' our director told me later, presumably meaning 'natural', 'honest', and 'without cunning or deceit'. But what I found even more compelling about the work in that classroom was the fact that their scenes were completely silent. Not a word was spoken, yet in my head, I was convinced they were all talking all the time. I felt that I could read their thoughts and see their intentions entirely in the way they moved.

I was astonished at my ability to empathise with these masks, particularly as they were all so crude. Huge, round balloon heads stuck on a child's body look grotesque and ridiculous. I remember feeling distinctly uncomfortable at first, but these feelings melted away the moment I saw them interacting in a simple situation. I empathised with the masks immediately because they were played so *simply*. Their movement was so completely natural because they had no one telling them what to do. We drama students always seemed to have someone telling us what to do, even amongst ourselves, but these kids looked so comfortable and relaxed with each other that their work looked effortless.

Those three girls with their scruffy school bag knew exactly what they were doing. Clearly, they were *improvising*. I very much doubt they'd have had the skill to reproduce their work with any accuracy – but that's not the point. I envied them their freedom and I envied the pleasure they found in the work. Angry Mum was really frightening, and you could see that she loved playing that anger. The Wayward Schoolgirl could hardly have been more rebellious, or more vulnerable. I thought she was trembling in terror all the way through. And I honestly thought that the Old Woman with the smiley face was going to burst into tears, until I realised she was far more interested in saving her lunch. The facial expressions had told me one thing; the body language had told me something else; but the reality revealed something different again.

The children in their 'art class' (if that was what they called it) clearly had ownership over what they were doing. They were pleasing themselves, rather than their teacher, working to their own taste, from their own experience, and reacting to each other without direction or censure from anyone else. They were completely confident with the choices they were making. But the word 'choices' implies a conscious element of interpretation. Although I'm completely convinced they knew exactly what they were doing, I'm not remotely convinced that they'd thought about it. This wasn't a structured rehearsal. They were just playing. I doubt they'd have made any distinction between what they were doing in their classroom that morning, and what they'd be doing in the playground that afternoon. They weren't trying to 'get it right' or to please anyone anyone other than themselves. It was the sheer fun of the work that made it so alive.

As far as playing masks was concerned, they were just doing what they thought people with faces like that would do. But there was considerable skill behind all that fun. At least, it's *skill* to those of us who value play, and it's a skill that's easily washed away with a year or so of formal education. I don't suppose your average Ofsted inspector would have approved of that lesson at all. Thankfully, they didn't exist in those days.

I know it sounds pretentious, but if I've ever had an 'epiphany' moment, that was it. Until then, I'd always thought that the text, and what you had to say, was more important than what you did, but by the time I was wheeling that mirror down the corridor, I was convinced that the opposite was also true, and that, in the right circumstances, action really does speak louder than words.

Later, when we talked about it, my colleagues were less enthusiastic: 'You can't make comparisons,' they said, no doubt exasperated with my continually banging on about it. 'They're kids. They don't know what they're doing.' And in any case, they were using masks, and masks are 'different', someone said. Masks had never been mentioned in our training other than in a historical context, and this remark brought a general consensus to the group. Those kids might have been excellent in their playing, but their use of masks made them 'different'. No one explored what was meant by being 'different', and I had no other frame of reference, because that was the only mask-work I'd seen; and because masks clearly *are* 'different', no useful comparison could be made between us. As a result, my observations were of no consequence. But in my mind, the fact remained that those kids were better than we were, and I wanted to know why. Why were masks different? And I also wanted to know how I could make theatre that was more like theirs – with masks or without.

Those kids had never heard of the Dreyfus brothers, and because they were working instinctively and weren't consciously trying to follow any rules or preconceived processes, they were all 'experts'. They all knew exactly what they were doing. The situation was crystal clear to them.

They knew the characters intimately, and they were driven more by their own sense of fun than any desire to 'get it right'. They weren't remotely interested in trying to be credible. They were just playing in the here-and-now. In other words, they all knew the characters they were playing by the masks, and they all knew the situation. Their game was to provoke each other, and in doing so, to make the situation worse. Tipping out the contents of the school bag on to the floor could hardly have been a bigger provocation to the Angry Mum; the Wayward Schoolgirl most likely went way beyond where she might go in real life – but that's the power of fiction. And everyone could empathise with the problems of living with an Angry Mum like that. In spite of the fact that they all looked as if they'd come from Mars, the drama of making a fuss about leaving the house on a school day could hardly have been more real. But it was their taste for provoking bigger and bigger reactions from each other, and pushing the situation to extremes, that generated the scene, and ultimately gave them ownership of what they were doing.

'The Holy Trinity'

We invent rules to make things happen. Our ability to do something as open and spontaneous as the action in the Tomato-Sandwich Incident boils down to a particular set of circumstances. Masks facilitate play, but if the following circumstances aren't firmly in pace, that playfulness will be stifled and eventually snuffed out. Call them rules if you like, but when these factors are in place you'll be able to play instinctively whether you're using masks or not.

1. Have nothing to remember.

2. Find the game.

3. Suck it and see.

This is 'the holy trinity' of instinctive play. But from the moment I see these three elements as 'rules', I'm constantly trying to find a way of breaking them without losing the empowerment and spontaneity they inspire.

It doesn't matter how you get to your understanding of the story you're in. That rehearsal was yesterday, and if you're trying to accurately reproduce what you were told to do yesterday, you're only doing 'choreography'. But if you *don't* remember what you did yesterday, the work will be lost and you'll be wasting everybody's time. It's appalling to be told that it looks as though you've been told to do something. But if your reactions are apparently instinctive, alive and playful, we'll see *you*, as opposed to seeing your instructions: the scene will capture our imagination, and you'll be playing.

I'm talking about a playfulness that emerges from reacting intuitively. By 'instinct' I mean that innate part of human behaviour that emerges without training, education or systematic rigorous textual analysis. That isn't to say that analysis is unhelpful; on the contrary. But it's worth considering how we may approach it.

'Have nothing to remember'

I once asked a Balinese dancer what he was thinking about when he played a mask.

'I breathe the mask, the mask breathes me,' he replied. 'I dance the mask, the mask dances me.'

'Do you remember what you did in the mask afterwards?'

'I am not there,' he told me, more in compassionate astonishment at my ignorance then in an attempt to patronise me about it.

'He was Jauk,' my interpreter, Wyan, tactfully reminded me then. ('Jauk' is the name of a traditional Balinese mask.) 'Jauk is very powerful,' he said, nodding wisely to himself.

This understanding of mask-work is a million miles away from anything a performer of my acquaintance might have told me in the West. This young Balinese man, sitting on a wall in the temple, drying his face with a towel, regarded the mask he'd recently been playing as a living entity in its own right. For him, the mask had its own intentions, its own desires and its own preferences. He gave the impression that the mask had 'taken him over' by mutual agreement, and now, in the warm haze of a jungle afternoon, he took no responsibility for what had happened.

But in the context of playing masks, 'having nothing to remember' is dangerously close to the common belief that masks induce 'trance' and 'out of mind' experiences. According to Keith Johnstone, in his seminal book *Impro* (Methuen 1979), 'A mask is a device for driving the personality out of the body and allowing a spirit to take possession of it.'

Alit, the performer and mask-maker I was working with in Bali during the eighties and nineties, would agree with that statement unreservedly, but it bears no relation to my experience of using masks, and it bears no relation to what those kids were doing in their big balloon heads.

But no self-respecting Balinese artist, be they a dancer, painter, musician, sculptor, or a even a child making a lucky charm, would dream of doing anything creative unless they were literally out of their minds. They practise Balinese Hinduism in Bali, and every aspect of life there has a religious element to it. Mask-work is a prime example. Masks are largely used to embody spiritual deities and to enable the gods to walk on earth amongst the people, and the Balinese use masks to make everyone remember that.

Bali has the only living tradition of mask theatre in the world; a tradition that goes back, in an unbroken line, to the eleventh century. Tiny shards of similar traditions can be found in other parts of Indonesia, and we find evidence that similar traditions of masks and trance were once practised in Haiti, Sri Lanka, and in various parts of Africa and Alaska.

But the notion that mask-work induces trance is deeply uncomfortable in our own culture. It might be interesting in the context of arcane religious practice, but for us, art is a very conscious affair. Masks aren't gods but devices to inspire playfulness. Trance is simply not on the menu, and the more you have to remember, the more inhibited that playfulness will be.

The idea that the best mask-work is always played in a state of trance is simply not true. Trance is no more a direct result of mask-work than waving a handkerchief might be of morris dancing. In the West we don't value things that put us out of control. We admire conscious and demonstrable skill. We value causality, reason and logic, and mask-work, in our culture, is more about inspiring playfulness than giving us an out-of-mind experience.

Having said all that, it's true that full-masks change the way we see the world. It's no wonder that the young Balinese dancer I was talking to got the feeling that he wasn't there. My son, at the age of seven, made much the same comment. After playing a mask for the first time, he told me earnestly that you get the feeling that you're 'not there'. I've heard academics refer to this feeling as 'absence', but I'm not convinced that you're remotely absent – quite the reverse. From behind the mask, when you see us react to you so strongly, even though you know perfectly well that you haven't done anything at all, you'll feel anything *but* absent. In fact, you'll be demonstrably 'there', watching us, through the eyeholes of the mask, and observing your own disappearance.

Transformation, anonymity, and a mischievous feeling of sheer delight at the realisation that you can make us react just by looking at us could hardly be more empowering. These are the elements that converge to change you in ways beyond your immediate control, but the jolting memory that you're supposed to be playing a 'doctor', for instance, destroys the immediacy of playing the mask because it's straining to have an effect. On the other hand, if you have nothing to remember in the first place, you'll hardly be able to stop yourself from reacting, the moment you catch sight of us from behind the mask.

Those kids in their big balloon heads had nothing to remember. They were far too preoccupied with making each other react to be bothered with anything else. They'd probably never seen a masked play before and didn't even know they were in one, but they stuck to their situation perfectly – until the tomato sandwich made its entrance. At that point everything was forgotten. But the fact is: they knew their situation so well that they had nothing to remember. They could all see how frightening Angry Mum was, and how provocative the Wayward Schoolgirl could be. The masks were perfect prompts for the situation, and the briefest glimpse of a face was enough to remind everyone of where we were and what was happening, while the action was kept alive through direct provocations, like emptying the school bag on the floor or slamming the shoe on the table.

For many of those kids, that conflict with the Angry Mum must have been very close to personal experience. If you're playing something outside your personal experience, you can't beat good old-fashioned research to gain an understanding of the world you're in. But even then, your credibility in the scene is more dependent on how that world affects you: What impulses do you get from your experience? How does it make you react?

Masks put ideas, feelings, attitudes and personal history neatly into a face. At least, that's what we like to think – but it's what you do that tells us who you are. In the Tomato-Sandwich Incident, the masks defined the situation and put the action in a context, but each action at the same time implied the thoughts and the feelings behind the faces. The face gives us the type, but the action implies who we think you are. Had the Angry Mum burst into tears rather than slamming the shoe on the table, the story would have changed completely, and our admiration of the Wayward Schoolgirl would have instantly evaporated.

The Tomato-Sandwich Incident has stuck in my mind for so long because it was my first experience of mask-work, and it was astonishingly credible to watch. Had any of that work looked remotely imposed – had any of those kids looked as if they'd been told to 'do it like that', or if they'd been merely illustrating what they wanted us to feel – I'd have seen the artifice immediately, and the masks would have looked crude and ineffectual. Thankfully, though, they were simply playing for themselves. They didn't have a director. They were simply entertaining themselves and could do what they liked. But the audience knew exactly what was happening. They all knew that it couldn't possibly be real. It was no more realistic than a cartoon, but at the same time everyone recognised exactly what they were dealing with here. They knew the characters, and they knew the situation, but because the characters couldn't talk, the audience's ability to read the body language instantly slipped into overdrive, and (certainly by everyone's reaction) the actors were astonishingly eloquent, in spite of the fact that they couldn't have been much older than nine or ten years old.

The audience always does most of the work in relating to masks. It's a fact of life, particularly in the silent world of a full-mask.

It's worth remembering here that masks don't inspire you to *act*, so much as make you *react*, and like it or not, you invariably end up playing a distorted version of yourself when you play a mask. To us on the outside, acting is the game of pretending to be someone else, and the stage is the only place, in our culture, where such a thing is acceptable. In fact, we expect pretence to happen there, and particularly if you're playing a mask. It's a foregone conclusion, even if you're still at primary school, like those kids in their big balloon heads: they all knew who the actors were, and who the audience were, and that what they were watching was all 'put on' to have an effect.

Some people balk at the word 'pretence' because, after all, it's 'feigned behaviour' and 'make-believe'. They regard acting as being more serious and profound than that. Some actors prefer terms like 'being (or 'becoming') someone else' to described what they do. But these are only metaphors to inform an idea of credible transformation. When you're on stage pretending to be someone else, the 'transformation' happens more in *our* heads (as the audience) than it does in *yours* (as an actor). You don't literally change your state of being the moment we find you credible. Those primary-school kids were perfectly credible and yet they were definitely and obviously 'pretending'. They were pretending so well that, in my head at least, they'd 'become' the people they were playing – despite the fact that the 'masks' were made out of paper cut-outs, and far too crude to be remotely real. But because they knew the situation perfectly and because their provocations were so clear, their playfulness, their desire to do things purely for the fun of it, was so refreshing that I believed them completely.

They hadn't been rehearsed, of course, and I doubt they'd have the ability to repeat what they'd found if they had been. The moment you do someone else's bidding in a mask, we'll see it immediately. The moment you're confused, unsure of yourself, or simply trying to tough it out, we'll see that too. But we'll also see those moments when you're really enjoying yourself. These moments tend to be more memorable because they're bolder, more daring, more admirable and more playful. You can't play when you've got something to remember, and clumsy direction soon pushes you into 'acting', so it's very easy to end up either ignoring the mask completely, or rebelling against the text. You can play anything you like in a mask, but if we're going to believe what you're doing, it has to be played in the manner inspired by the mask. Or to be more accurate, it has to be done *without you getting in the way*.

In the West our theatre is based more on what's written down than on any notion of masking. In our culture it's simplistic to think that, no matter how instinctive and how compelling effective mask-work might be, it can't possibly rival the emotional and intellectual capacity of a carefully structured piece of dramatic literature. This book isn't an attempt to debunk this idea and promote mask-work for its own sake. My interest in the subject lies in exploring those places where the mask and the text meet and inform each other.

Telling you to 'have nothing to remember' is a fatuous thing to insist on. Of course, you've always got something to remember! But playing a mask whilst going through conventional processes of text analysis and conventional interpretive rehearsal processes will put you in a situation where one set of impulses might cancel out another. Contrary to popular opinion, playing a mask isn't the same as playing a 'character'. When you play a mask in a dramatic situation you're not so much assuming a role as changing the casting. You're too busy coping with the impulses inspired by the mask to remember who you're supposed to be. And it's then that you must 'find the game'.

'Finding the game'

Any action can be turned into a game at the moment you admit to yourself that you're doing it purely for effect, to provoke a reaction for the fun of it. All dramatic action is there to provoke something. Even a simple activity like standing a little closer to someone than you would normally do, or looking intently at someone, or else not looking at them at all: all these actions, in the right context, can become very provocative games. 'Finding the game' is my way of asking you to identify what you want to do and to find the fun in doing it. Some people refer to this as 'finding your objective', which is a much more complex activity, with a lot to remember. Regardless of what you want in a scene, though, you're always 'playing' for it. That play is a game, and the moment you acknowledge it's a game, rather than a serious dramatic obligation, the action comes alive, and becomes spontaneous. Choices emerge and you feel more empowered to take risks. Sometimes you have the freedom to play anything, just for the fun of it, but most situations are tightly structured with a set of circumstances that determine the type of game required, and the effect you're trying to have on the others in the scene.

Games can be declared or hidden. If you're showing us that what your doing is a game, you're 'declaring' it and potentially taking us into your confidence. If we like the game and understand what you mean by it, we'll accept it for what it is, and openly collude with you to make it more effective. If, on the other hand, we don't know any of these things and are invited simply to accept what you're doing as if it were real, then you're *hiding the game*. But it's still a game. Even if you're plumbing the depths of nineteenth-century naturalism, it's still no more than an elaborate game. All stage action is a game played for effect.

The Wayward Schoolgirl emptying the contents of her satchel out in the middle of the floor in the Tomato-Sandwich Incident, the Angry Mum slamming a shoe on the desk – these were both distinct provocations to keep the game alive, but they *were* both games. Games are endemic in effective action.

My insistence on 'finding the game' is an attempt to encourage you to identify the action and to give you something to play. Reducing acting to a series of games sounds simplistic but simple ideas are generally the best. By definition, *play* needs to be simple. Complex ideas make difficult games that give you too much to remember.

Peter Hall's 1993 Old Vic production of *Lysistrata* was performed in half-masks, but the quality of the mask-work was such that I ended up asking myself why they were using masks in the first place. Why have them if you re not going to play them? Mask-work doesn't sit easily with conventional literary processes. I understood every word of that production, but all I saw was the acting. In Bali I watched countless mask plays and never understood a word of them, but I could always see exactly why the masks were there – because the masks were being played with as much care as the text.

In one of my early attempts to come to terms with half-masks, I remember an exchange with the young Phelim McDermott, who was playing a particularly angry and aggressive half-mask.

'Try coming on and leaning casually on the back of the chair and relaxing a bit,' I suggested.

'So you want me,' he said in a softly aggressive tone, 'to come on "casually", like this and – ' he demonstrated – 'then to "relax", and – '

he demonstrated again. 'No. To... "ree-lax".' And he demonstrated another more ridiculous way of relaxing. He was rolling all over the floor by this stage. 'You want me to do all that on the back of that chair?' And with that he burst out laughing. 'Are you serious?' He was strutting about the set now – and playing the mask magnificently.

There are two radically different theatrical conventions clashing with each other here: the convention of an actor following the director's instructions; and the convention of the actor 'finding the game' in the situation provided. In this instance, my attempts at direction became *provocations*, and this incident taught me a lesson I have never forgotten. Had I insisted on what I wanted, Phelim would barely have been able to play the mask at all, and we would probably have felt obliged to stop the game.

If you treat the masks as the characters in a play, and try to apply conventional techniques of text analysis and rational choices, rather than going for deliberate provocation, you'll immediately be in danger of giving everyone far too much to remember, and we in the audience will all be asking 'Why use masks?' because we always want to see masks go further than we do in real life. We want to see them being *more* spontaneous, *more* daring and *more* mischievous than any of us would ever dare to be, unmasked. Or else we want to see them braver than we dare to imagine possible. We want to see them suffer, triumph, and overcome adversity. 'Finding the game' and direct provocation go hand in hand. The techniques of provoking half-masks to shock you into a spontaneous reaction is a skill you can apply in other aspects of theatre-making – provided everyone concerned is prepared to 'find the game'.

There's a huge difference between 'remembering' and 'playing'. When you 'play' you don't have to remember, because playing turns everything you do into a game. And the game of pretending that you know exactly what you're doing is very popular. Once you know what you're doing, action pops into your head with the smallest impulse. When you really 'know' the text, you don't have to remember either, because words and actions bring a strong personal resonance to the writing. Once you've experienced a situation to the extent that you respect the feelings it puts you through, you can exploit these resonances and play with them. Suddenly you're in a position to push against the fixed parameters of the scene and to raise the stakes. That's the power of playfulness.

In the film *My Left Foot*, Daniel Day-Lewis played the writer and painter Christy Brown, and as part of his research he befriended a quadriplegic patient in a hospital in Ireland who had the same condition as the character in the film. He wanted to study the appalling restrictions this patient had to live with. The story goes that while on set, during filming, he committed himself so completely to this assumed physicality that he refused to emerge from his wheelchair to get on to the set. The technicians had to lift him, in his chair, over the cables. I wonder if they helped him in the bathroom as well. It's reported that he held this twisted posture so hard and for so long that he ended up breaking a rib in the process. To my mind, there's more to creative representation than a detailed copy of real life.

Daniel Day-Lewis's renowned obsession with recreating reality, and the hard toll his accuracy and diligence took on his body, might be considered a fair price to pay for the brilliant quality of the performance that emerged. And yet, famously, during a National Theatre production of *Hamlet*, the actor suddenly imagined that he was seeing his own father on stage, and was so disturbed by this vision that he had to withdraw from the production. Irrespective of the meticulous research he had undertaken to play the Prince, his own father had recently died.

Credible acting has a strong affinity with actuality, and actuality puts everything firmly in the here-and-now. And yet when push comes to shove, we all know that what happens on stage isn't real. It would appear that Daniel Day-Lewis was not in an appropriate state of mind to appreciate this duality. Play has its own reality, but it's exactly because play is frivolous, and so apparently inconsequential, that it enables you to take more risks: to be bolder in your choices and to challenge values you've been brought up to take for granted. Play enables you to raise the stakes far higher in a particular situation than you'd ever do in real life.

Stephen Harper is an astonishingly playful actor, with years of experience in playing masks. He was in the original cast of *War Horse* at the National Theatre. As part of their early rehearsal process, a Regimental Sergeant Major was brought in to teach them army drill. After some time of marching about and standing to attention, Steve was beginning to find the experience somewhat joyless, so on a mischievous impulse he stepped out of line and slapped the peak of the Sergeant Major's cap. The RSM's response was instantaneous. He bellowed a tirade of abuse at Steve, inches away from his face. Steve told me he was so shocked and overwhelmed by the experience that he was almost in tears when it finally stopped. But after that incident the drill was pursued with a genuine vigour by everyone involved.

In the bar, after rehearsal, the Sergeant Major thanked Steve sincerely for what he'd done, because his action had brought the event to life. Before that moment, the RSM told him, he felt he'd merely been going through the motions of 'drilling a cast of actors', but Steve's provocation had given the whole process more meaning for everyone involved. Steve's natural proclivity towards playfulness over choreography, and provocation over blind obedience, brought him, quite literally, face to face with old-fashioned army discipline. Once a game becomes interlaced in the dramatic circumstances, your action generates its own reality.

The moment you turn 'what you want' in a scene into a game, Dee Cannon's' 'Ten Commandments' become parameters that can contain and shape your playfulness. Games bring the dramatic circumstances alive. In this case, Steve's abrupt provocation, his playful aggression, brought a dreary session of military drill for a group of pretend soldiers instantly to life for everyone involved. It turned a repetitive rehearsal into an event in itself. Actuality in a fictional event – by which I mean everything that's 'real' – generates a strong feeling of personal ownership, if only because *you were there*. Empiricism is invaluable because it gives us a personal understanding of what happened. By comparison, any attempt to consciously imitate that reality, even if you break a rib in the process, is shamefully superficial. But games are for real. You're not asked to act or to recreate anything. You either play the game or you don't.

But simply following someone else's instructions isn't 'play': it's obedience. Similarly, articulating choices decided days beforehand isn't 'play': it's interpretation. Play is apparently spontaneous and essentially meaningless. Play thrives on its ability to have an effect on other people. Of course, we don't trust meaningless elements in a scene: we deride them as blatant stupidity. Thankfully, though, meaningless action is difficult to sustain and soon evaporates, allowing our taste for things that we understand, and empathise with, to bubble to the surface.

People don't trust play because they can't direct it. You can provoke it with games, and channel it through dramatic situations, but if you try to break it down, or control it by 'actioning the text', 'articulating your internal monologue', 'stating your objective' and continually referring back to the 'given circumstances', the more likely you'll be to kill the flame. 'They're obsessed with fucking meaning,' Cicely Berry once muttered in my ear during a mask session at the RSC, and she was right. But as Peter Brook once said: 'The work of rehearsal is to find the meaning and make it meaningful.' In other words, you don't know what that meaning is before you start. Play is an innate ability, which we all share, to do things purely for effect: to entertain, frighten or surprise each other.

I respect Daniel Day-Lewis, and I admire his diligence; but playfulness is a discipline that's just as robust as the most diligent research. Accurate imitations of reality make earnest demands on everyone involved. The entire team is obliged to submit to them because you believe you're unassailably in the right. But fidelity to reality soon becomes drudgery. It's never enough just to mimic reality; you have to recreate it in a way that best serves the writing and the audience you're playing to. Daniel Day-Lewis was doing all these things, but his lack of playfulness, and his denial of the game, eventually tipped him into delusion, and any notion of pretense was completely lost on him.

'Suck it and see'

Those old imperatives of wanting to 'get it right', wanting to be good, and wanting to be seen to be good, are the biggest obstacles to sustained playfulness. Your imaginative drive comes to an abrupt end the moment you start to berate yourself for not being good enough, not knowing what to do, or feeling inadequate. 'Suck it and see' is a tacit invitation to provoke: to do something, out of the blue. It's the desire to make something else happen, to take a risk, to break the existing rules and do something daring. The entrance of the tomato sandwich is a prime example of what I'm talking about. On the one hand it stopped the drama, and on the other it abruptly took everything in an entirely different direction. You could say that it was an absurd intervention that trashed everything, but it was also an incident that gave everyone concerned a fresh new starting point. Phelim's refusal to take my direction was also a 'suck it and see' moment. He was giving vent to an abrupt impulse to be outrageous: to toss convention aside and cut against the grain.

'Suck it and see' is that irresponsible aspect of play that gives instinctive behaviour its bad reputation. Like trance, we don't trust irrational impulses, but very few people are wantonly destructive. If you're trying to be spontaneous, it's understandable that you might do something in a rush of adrenalin that can't be justified after the event, and that you later regret. But in a world of outrageous pretence like this one, nobody dies. In this world, triumphs are exciting, but catastrophes have so much more to teach. I remember Philippe Gaulier, when confronted by an eager and ambitious group of would-be Clowns, saying: 'Those of you who fail miserably will be taken out and punished. Those of you who succeed and are very good will be punished in exactly the same way. In fact, it will be worse for you. Guilt can be made to last for ever.'

We all laughed, of course, more out of embarrassment than understanding. But the more that failure and success are disregarded, the less likely it will be that that impulse to do something, just to see what happens, will end up being destructive.

'The holy trinity' – 'Have nothing to remember', 'Find the game', and 'Suck it and see' – will give you the ideal conditions for generating play. Regardless of what you look like, and who we think you are, seeing you react in the volatile circumstances of a game will always reveal more than you're aware of. Behind a mask, you're like a learner driver, incapable of seeing beyond the end of the bonnet. But we on the outside can see right down to the end of the road because we know exactly what you look like, and we can't wait to see how your provocations and reactions will inspire a change in you. It could be admiration, empathy, respect, derision or even contempt. But because you're totally unaware of what we think about you, the game is unabated.

From the outside, masks confront us with questions about who we think you are. But behind the mask, when you've got nothing to remember, and you're ready to 'find the game' and be fully prepared to 'suck it and see', your mind is focused on more immediate imperatives than your intention, or your super-objective, or your character. On the outside, that mask might make you look outrageous or even ridiculous: 'No normal, real-live human being, looks like *that*!' And as a result we give your wildest impulses instantly validity. 'That's what you do where you come from,' we think to ourselves, and we applaud your audacity, and love to see you trashing convention, because, deep down, we think you're playing to a different set of rules. You could be an entirely different species, as far as we're concerned.

Having the confidence and the apparent recklessness to 'suck it and see', and take a risk, opens up the irresponsible and uncertain world of chance and imaginative speculation that pulls the rug away from under our feet. This is a world where we're all playing, if only to see what's going to happen next. It's a place where the effects of the game you've just started are yet to be found.

The Only Rule of Theatre

If you temporarily remove the notion that theatre is an illusion of reality; if you take away the requirement to recreate psychology, abandon the convention that theatre-making is primarily a literary skill, and abolish the 'Ten Commandments', you'll be left with nothing more than you, the audience, and a restless imagination. This is the starting point of the **expert**. This is a world where you can do what you want, provided we find you interesting. Here, the only rule of theatre is *Don't be boring*; and it's the only rule worth remembering, and the only one that really matters. There are always subsidiary rules, of course, or you'd never be able to define your conventions, but all these subsidiary rules are optional. You can make something as real, and as beautiful as you like. You can make it replete with meaning, dripping in emotion, or full to the brim with political relevance, but the moment it drifts into boredom… you're dead. It might be inane and ridiculous, but if we're laughing, or simply watching you with undivided attention, you'll know we're not bored. But even if we react with mockery and outrage, this is preferable to the dead hand of boredom.

But 'suck it and see' isn't a call to anarchy, because we can't function without any rules at all. Every new game is a different set of rules. And every time we remove one set of rules, we can't help ourselves imposing another. All I'm trying to do here is make a plea for honesty. An idea might have worked brilliantly when it first occurred to you. It might have really rung a bell at the time. But if that bell doesn't ring any more, it's worth remembering that you're not committing an act of idolatry by doing something else.

Stanislavsky and Copeau weren't gurus. Neither of them had 'the secret to a happy life' or the secret to flawless acting, any more than you or I do. They simply had more questions than they knew what to do with. It's this desire to know something that makes their work compelling to us today.

I admire their tenacity, their perception and their steely determination to make something different. But more than that, I admire their ability to make choices for themselves. Like the guru in the story I started this chapter with, they were chancers, playing hunches and thinking on their feet. They trusted their own judgements rather than those of anyone else; but even then, they only *thought* they knew. They were essentially just making it up as they went along. Approach anything in this way and you suddenly have a bigger space to play in. Gurus might be excellent to have around, if you're religious, but gurus in art are a deadly idea. 'Oh but *so-and-so* was brilliant in *such-and-such*, and *so-and-so* trained with *so-and-so* as well.' We know nothing at all about that relationship.

Stanislavsky and Copeau were speculating with starting points and creative ideas. They weren't dealing with natural laws. They weren't scientists. Acting isn't a science so much as an Olympian feat of the imagination. Stanislavsky might have been dazzled by the emerging science of psychology, but psychology is so much yesterday's news. The only similarity between him and Freud was their indomitable curiosity.

The Trickster (page 185)

Man About To Be Hero (page 196)

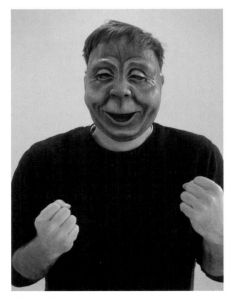

The Fool (page 205)

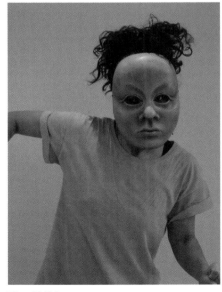

The Child (page 213)

The Virgin (page 216)

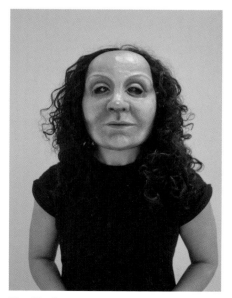

The Mother (page 219)

The Huntress (page 223)

The Ogre (page 226)

The Crone (page 228)

The Hermit (page 231)

The Devil (page 236)

Naïve Masks (page 254)